THE CURIOUS SCI

A Series by Deepak, Ananya, an

Illustrated by Katie Risor

Jackets and Genes

First Edition

Hardcover ISBN: 978-1-68515-230-7
Paperback ISBN: 978-1-68515-231-4
eBook ISBN: 978-1-68515-232-1

Library of Congress Control Number: 2021924326

Place of publication: San Diego, CA
The Curious Scholars LLC

Illustation Copyright © 2022 Katie Risor
www.katierisor.com

Dear Grandma,

... our forever Love!

... and the genetic code for affection,

kindness and everything beautiful!

DEAR TEACHERS AND PARENTS,

Thank you for choosing this book!

"Jackets and Genes" is the first in a four-book series that will introduce your child to the exciting world of genes, DNA, and everything that makes genetics so amazing!

As parents and teachers, we often struggle to explain the many fundamental concepts around biological sciences. Our impromptu science discussions about genes, viruses and vaccines, during the pandemic lockdown, eventually became this book about *Casey, Anika, Thomas and Gabriella* learning about genetics. We wrote *"Jackets and Genes"* together as a fun introduction to genes for children, roughly for the highly motivated 8-year-old to - 14 years' age range. We wanted to instruct scientific knowledge in language that's accessible to late elementary and middle schoolers so that children can establish a firm foundation of scientific impressions for a future where applied genomics will increasingly become more and more mainstream.

Some of the concepts this book will introduce to your child include: *What are genes? What is a DNA? What are chromosomes? Where do the genes, DNA, and chromosomes live in the body? Do only humans have genes? What do genes really do? What is a phenotype? What is a genotype? Finally, the book provides a perspective about* **what makes us all so similar but just as much unique!**

Even though two of the authors of this book are children themselves, we strongly recommend that adults read "Jackets and Genes" alongside their kids, to explain any concepts that prove complicated for them to grasp. To better understand the concepts, a glossary of terms based on National Human Genome Research Institute, has been provided. We see this as a staple of the bookshelf, with kids (and their parents!) coming back to it again and again when needed.

As you read, look out for hidden codes in the book—like the names of the main characters, which begin with the same letters as the basic units that make up DNA and genes (the letter "U" is scheduled to make an appearance in subsequent books!), appearance of Griffin, a labradoodle to introduce that genes are important in animals too, and presence of gnomes as an introductory plot for the next book title.

As your child progresses through this book series the scientific concepts will mature, with the characters advancing by two years in each of the follow up books. They grow with your kids, and become two years smarter and two years more learned.

The subsequent books in this scientific series, geared toward their pursuit include:

GNOMES AND GENOMES – This is where they will learn more details about genomes, Human Genome Project, gene libraries, gene sequencing, and much more.

COPY AND PASTE – This book will teach your child about the basics of transcription, translation, protein synthesis, and what keeps the genetic material intact through generations.

EN'GENE'ERING AND MORE – This will cover some of the genetic engineering techniques that are used in applied genomics for treating diseases, forensics, and gene editing, and will provide more insight in addressing real world issues through genomics.

It is our hope this book and forthcoming inclusions in "The Curious Scholars" series will bring out the fantastic scientist that lies within your child.

And, while *"Jackets and Genes"* is an engaging and exciting read, it's academically rigorous as well: The lessons in this book have a focus on the standards of education set by the Next Generation of Science Standards, specifically MS-LS1 and HS-LS 1: From Molecules to Organisms: Structures and Processes.

And yes! feel free to send an email at contact@TheCuriousScholars. com to say a quick hello, send feedback or for bulk/library purchases. Check out http://www.TheCuriousScholars.com for more. So, let's dive in and help your child decode (no pun) the world of genes!

Sincerely yours,

Deepak Asudani
Ananya Asudani
Aarnav Asudani

TABLE OF CONTENTS

"Casey, your word is 'genes,'" Principal Newman announced.

Casey looked around nervously. He had made it to the finals of Oak Stone Norte Academy's annual spelling bee. It was down to him and Gabriella. If he answered this wrong, he'd lose! The trouble was, **he was stumped!** The only jeans he'd ever heard of were the ones that you wore. But that couldn't be the word Principal Newman was looking for. Could it?

"Is there an alternate pronunciation?" he asked.

"No, there are no other pronunciations," Principal Newman said.

"What part of speech is it?" Casey asked, hoping to get some hints.

"It is a noun," Principal Newman said.

"Can I please have it in a sentence?" Casey asked.

"There are around 25,000 different genes in a human body," said Principal Newman

Casey sighed. That hadn't helped at all. He would just have to guess. "Um, genes. J-E-A-N-S. Genes."

Principal Newman rang a bell. Ding. "I'm sorry, Casey. That is incorrect. The correct spelling is G-E-N-E-S."

Genes? Casey thought. What does that even mean?

Beside him, Gabriella got to spell her winning word. She correctly spelled the word jackets. "Jackets. J–A–C–K–E–T–S. Jackets," said Gabriella without much effort.

Ugh. Why couldn't I have gotten that one? Casey wondered.

"Congratulations on winning the spelling bee, Gabriella!" Anika said a few minutes later.

"Thanks," Gabriella replied happily. "But I wouldn't have won if I'd gotten Casey's word. What are genes, anyway?" The curious students sat on the steps and wondered.

"Principal Newman said it had to do with the human body," Thomas said. "That sounds like science. Let's ask Mrs. Love tomorrow."

"Good idea," replied Casey. "If I'm going to lose, I'd at least like to know what the word I lost on means!"

The next morning, Casey and his friends waited patiently for science class to start.

"Good morning students," Mrs. Love said. "Before we begin class, congratulations to our two amazing spellers, Gabriella, for winning, and Casey, for being the runner up. This class always makes me so proud!"

Casey raised his hand. "Mrs. Love, speaking of the spelling bee, we had a question for you. What are genes?"

"That's a good question, Casey, and it fits perfectly with today's lesson on the human body!" said Mrs. Love. "Think of genes like the words in an instruction manual. Just like the words tell you what to do, genes tell the **cells** in your body what to do."

Casey raised his hand again. "How do they do that? And where are our genes?" he asked.

"Well," Mrs. Love said, "As you know cells make up our body. The inside of those cells is called the **nucleus**. The nucleus holds long strands of DNA that are coiled very neatly and tightly into something called chromosomes. Each of us has 23 pairs of chromosomes. On these DNA strands, which make up the chromosomes, are scattered codes called 'genes'. I know it can be confusing, and you need to look at this cool picture I have that tells you more," said Mrs. Love.

"Let me also show you a fun way to describe it:

Deep within those tiny but mighty cells is nucleus
and inside that lie **Chromosomes***, 23 pairs of them!*
All these chromosomes are made up of **DNA***, the secret of life.*
And on the strands of DNA are the codes, what we call **genes***!*
These are much like treasure-hunt clues and recipes,
that must make **proteins***, several thousands of them!*
These proteins and other chemicals interact and go to work
to make you the **very special you!**

Gabriella raised her hand. "Do we ALL have chromosomes?" she asked.

"Yep," responded Mrs. Love, "And each of us has 23 pairs of chromosomes."

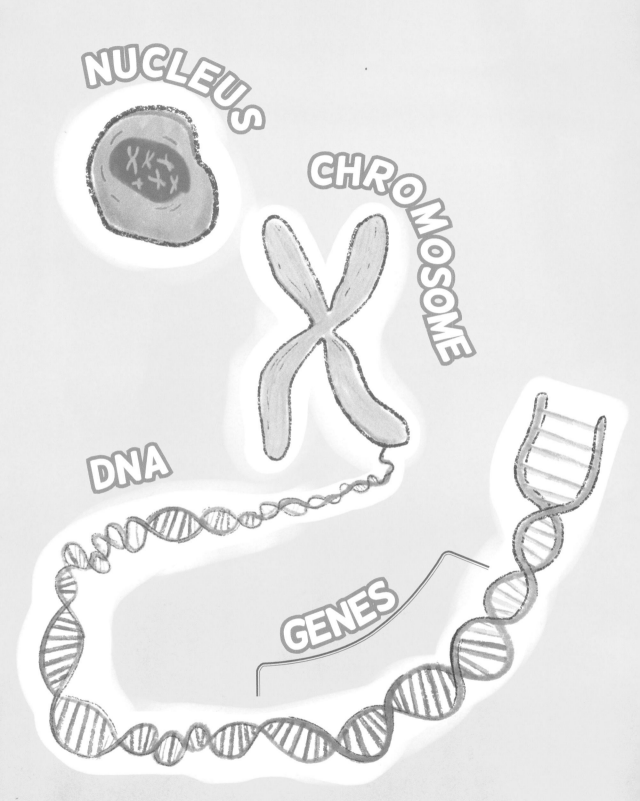

NUCLEUS

CHROMOSOME

DNA

GENES

19

"So if we all have the same number of chromosomes, why are we all not similar?", asked Gabriella curiously.

"Aha!" Mrs. Love replied. "Excellent question. That's because what is inside our chromosomes is not the same.

"And by the way, humans have 23 pairs of chromosomes, but different species have different numbers," Mrs. Love explained. "Your body is like a computer, and your genes are like the code that makes your body function," Mrs. Love smiled at the students. "Every living thing has a **genetic code**. Ninety-nine point nine percent of every human's genetic code is the same. But the remaining less than a tenth of one percent is different, and that small percent is what gives Thomas his curly hair and makes Casey's hair blonde and straight."

"Your genetic code is what makes you, You—the special YOU! Our genes tell our bodies how we should look. And they tell our bodies how to function. But the really cool part is that even though we humans look different, we are actually very similar!", she continued.

"Like how 'genes' in your body is spelled differently from the jeans you wear, and yet they are pronounced the same way?" Casey asked.

The class giggled, but Mrs. Love nodded. "Exactly, Casey! You are such a sport!"

"I think it's because of my baseball-playing dad. It must be all in the genes," Casey said again, to the class's delight.

"That must be what they mean when they say, 'The apple doesn't fall far from the tree,'" said Gabriella.

The class laughed again.

"This has already been such a fun day, class. You are the best!" exclaimed Mrs. Love.

Anika, who loved to summarize things, was paying close attention. Everyone was waiting for her to say her favorite phrase: "Just so that we are all clear." And, sure enough, Anika raised her hand.

"I think I see what you are saying, Mrs. Love. Just so that we are all clear, it's like the genes are a set of instructions that tell the cells what to do, how to do it, and when to do it, so that the cells do their jobs correctly."

"That's absolutely right, Anika," Mrs. Love said. "Now, since this class is full of such great spellers, I have a spelling challenge for you all," said Mrs. Love. "Who can spell DNA?"

"I'd win THAT spelling bee," Casey chortled. "D–N–A!"

"Ah, but you didn't let me finish, Casey," Mrs. Love said with a twinkle in her eye. "DNA is the acronym—the letters stand for 'Deoxyribo Nucleic Acid'!"

The class looked at Gabriella and Casey, who looked extremely lost at the thought of spelling those unpronounceable words.

Luckily, the bell chimed just in time, and just like that, class was over.

Mrs. Love looked at the students. "Oh my! Time flies fast. It's been such an amazing morning! And there's so much more to learn. If you want to know what genes look like, why don't you ask Mrs. Williams when you have art class this afternoon? You will be coming back to my class after you are done with Mrs. Williams' class"

"Cool!" said Casey.

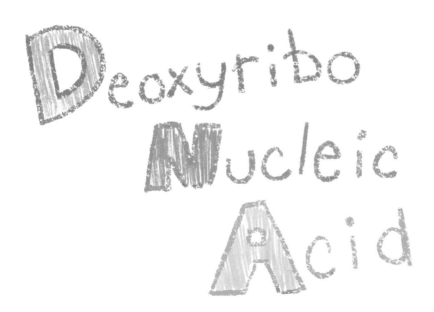

After lunch, the kids went to Mrs. Williams' art class. It was Thomas's favorite, because Thomas loved to doodle, draw and paint.

"Who's ready to paint some DNA?" Mrs. Williams asked.

Mrs. Williams and Mrs. Love were lunch buddies, and over their sandwiches in the break room, Mrs. Love had told Mrs. Williams all about the children's fascination with genes and the human body.

The kids waved their paintbrushes in the air.

"But how can we draw the DNA if we don't know what it looks like?" Gabriella asked.

"Just remember three things," Mrs. Williams said.

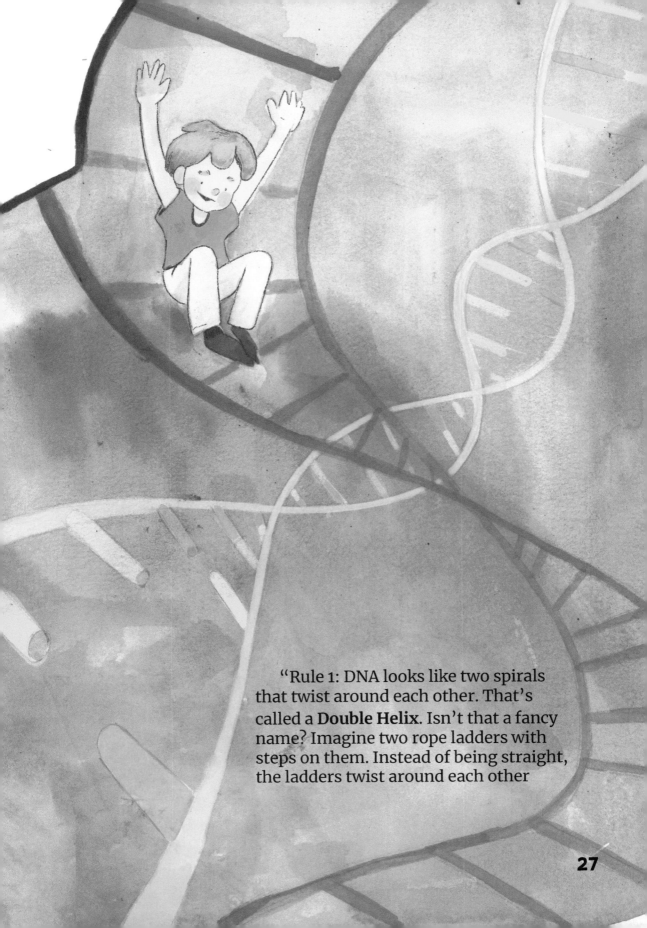

"Rule 1: DNA looks like two spirals that twist around each other. That's called a **Double Helix**. Isn't that a fancy name? Imagine two rope ladders with steps on them. Instead of being straight, the ladders twist around each other

"Rule 2: Each spiral step has letters attached to it.
"D–N–A?" guessed Anika.

"Good guess, but no—the letters are **A–C–G–T.**
     A stands for Adenine
          C stands for Cytosine
               G stands for Guanine
                    T stands for Thymine"

"What does that *mean*?" Anika asked.

"It's a lot, I know," Mrs. Williams sympathized. "All you need to know right now is that A, C, G and T refer to different kinds of chemicals that help make up what are known as **nucleotides**. Make sure you use a distinct color for each of these letters—I mean nucleotides.

Rule 3: Adenine always pairs with Thymine, and Guanine always pairs with Cytosine. It's like they're best friends that only hang out together. These are called **base pairs,** and when you paint them, you can paint as many as you want—just don't mix up the friends!"

"Just so we're clear," Anika chimed in, "it's a swirled around rope ladder, with stairs made up of **ACGT**. And A goes with T, and C with G. Right?" she asked.

"Just so we're clear!" her friends said in unison.

The kids got messy with their paints and canvases, and after what felt like no time at all, Mrs. Williams announced the end of class.

Casey looked at his painting. "I feel like a scientist!" he said enthusiastically.

The other kids agreed; their heads felt stuffed full of DNA and A–C–G–T and other science–y words. When they'd come to school that morning, they hadn't known anything about genes, and now they knew so much about the genes and DNA. They felt really smart.

The kids collected their masterpieces, and took them back to Mrs. Love's class.

"Look at the amazing paintings you made!" said Mrs. Love, looking impressed. "And it looks like Mrs. Williams told you about ACGT."

Gabriella nodded. "But what do those letters really do?" she asked.

" Oh yes, I need to tell you about those letters. And along the way I will be sharing some cool fun facts. A, C, G and T are what we call the building blocks of your cells," Mrs. Love explained. "Together they form your genes."

"So if we have 23 pairs of chromosomes," Thomas said— "in humans," Mrs. Love interjected. "Other species have different amounts."

"...then how many genes do we have?" he asked

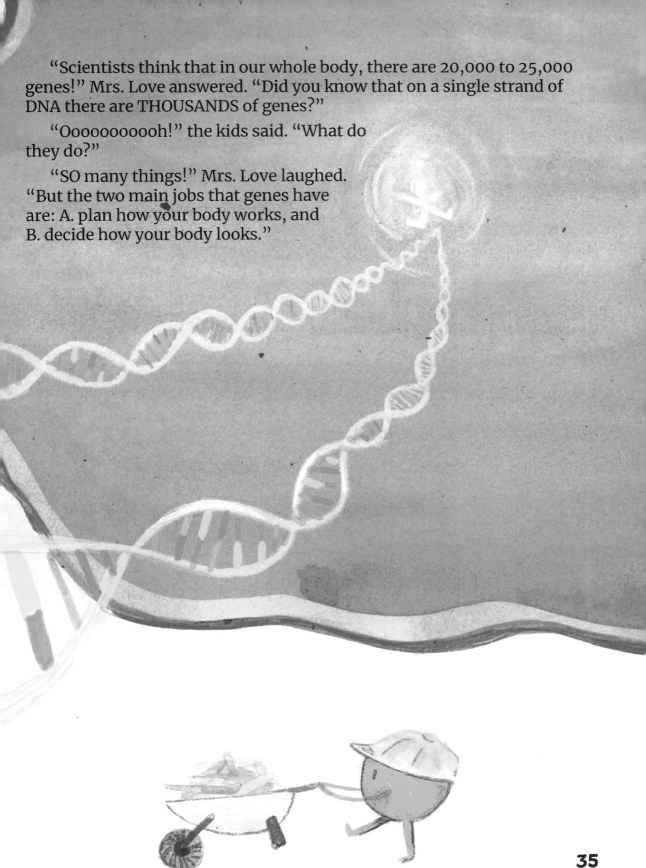

"Scientists think that in our whole body, there are 20,000 to 25,000 genes!" Mrs. Love answered. "Did you know that on a single strand of DNA there are THOUSANDS of genes?"

"Ooooooooooh!" the kids said. "What do they do?"

"SO many things!" Mrs. Love laughed. "But the two main jobs that genes have are: A. plan how your body works, and B. decide how your body looks."

"Let me ask you something. Has anyone ever assembled a desk or a bike before?" Mrs. Love enquired.

"Me, me, me!" Thomas shouted. "Last year my mom and I assembled a desk for my room."

"Excellent," Mrs. Love said. "Now, did you have to imagine in your head how to put the parts together all by yourself, without any help?"

"Of course not!" Thomas said excitedly. "It came with an "instruction manual" and we read the instructions together and then we figured out how to put the parts together."

"And how did the desk look, when you put it together?" Mrs. Love prompted. "Did it look like the black and white drawing in the manual?"

"Not at all!" Thomas said. "The desk was brown, not black and white. It was my size, not tiny like in the booklet, and I could actually put my books on it and everything."

"So what you did with your mom, Thomas," Mrs. Love said, "was to use a **genotype**—the instruction manual—to put together the **phenotype**—your brown desk! So think of your genes in the same way.

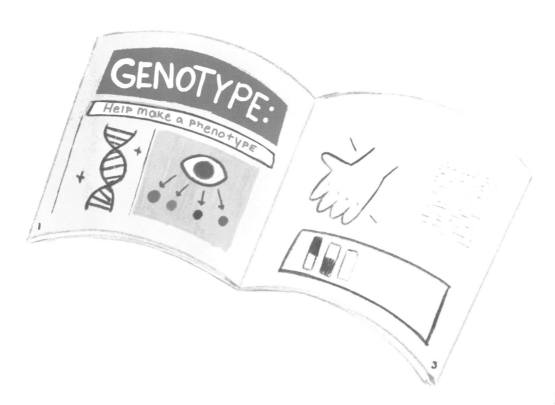

The genes determine a lot of things depending on the proteins they help make. Think of your outward appearance like a jacket you put on. You can look different when you put on different clothes, jackets, and jeans. These features and observable characteristics—called traits—determine how you look, your eye color, the shape of your ears, your smile, freckles, hair curls, and a lot more. That has a fancy name called a '**phenotype**.' In a lot of ways, our genes figure out how our outward physical characteristics are decided. This phenotype also depends to some extent on the environment. And the complete set of genes that we inherit from our parents is what we call a '**genotype**.' Basically, a genotype is all the genes in our DNA put together that we get from our parents.

Wow, I didn't know genes could be like desks!" exclaimed Gabriella.

"And that's not all! If you were assembling your desk, but realized you lost a screw or a rod, you'd have to go out and buy another, right?" Mrs. Love continued. "But the amazing thing about our genes is that if this happened to them, they could just MAKE. SOME. MORE!"

"Wow! So genes must be really very smart!" Gabriella said.

"Of course, just like you guys," Mrs. Love said with a laugh.

"Tell us more about genes: Are they big or small? Do they all do the same stuff?" asked Gabriella.

"Not at all! Mrs. Love answered. Some genes are small, and only have 300 base pairs of letters, but others can have a million.

39

FUN FACT

Genes help make **proteins**, which are the building blocks of everything in your body: your hair, your muscles, your bones, your teeth. Proteins like insulin and pepsin help digest food. These are called 'functional proteins.' Others help build things. Proteins like keratin and myosin make body structures. These are called 'structural proteins. What genes really do is tell the cells how to make all these proteins. It is these details that help cells decide whether you are going to have blue eyes or brown, whether you will have curled hair or straight, and to some degree, what kind of temperament you keep. And those dimples and freckles. Once the body has all these proteins available, they put them together so that our amazing bodies can do their function well. It's like putting together building blocks to make different structures.

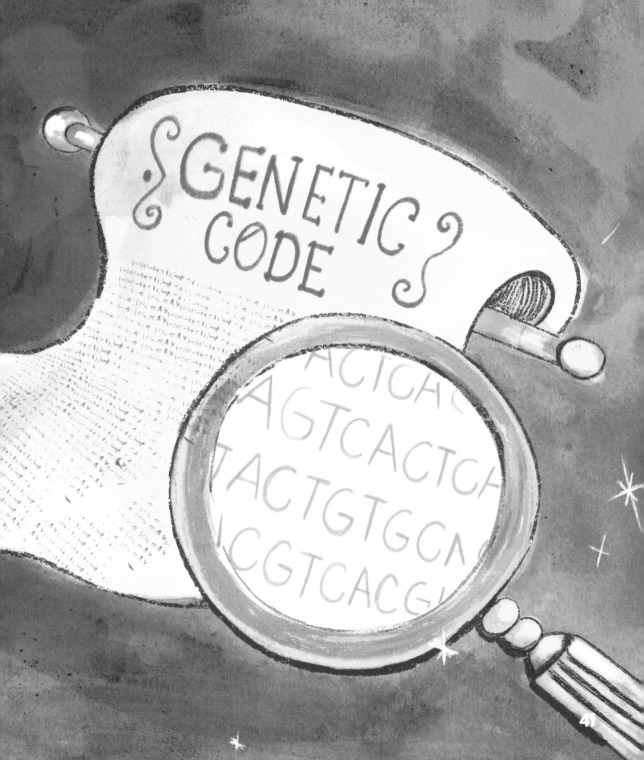

"That's awesome, said Gabriella.

"In fact, all living forms have genes that determine their individual characteristics," Mrs. Love shared.

"Wait, Mrs. Love, so does Griffin, our labradoodle, also have genes and DNA?" asked Anika.

"He absolutely does, Anika! It's not only human beings who have genes. Animals do, as do plants, bacteria, fungi, and viruses. All living things have genes and DNA."

"Oh wow! That's so exciting" Anika exclaimed.

"So, if all living things have genes, then why does an avocado look like an avocado and a sloth looks like a sloth?" asked Thomas.

"That's a great question, Thomas," said Mrs. Love. "All living things have genes, and they have lots of similarities, but it's the small differences that make us all unique. For example, 96 percent of genes of humans and chimpanzees are similar. It's that remaining four percent that makes us human and them chimpanzees. Isn't it amazing that with such a tiny difference, we can have such a large variety of creatures?"

"That's awesome," Casey agreed.

Mrs. Love nodded. "Here's another one. Some scientists say the similarity between humans and bananas is 50 percent. Go figure!"

"I'm confused about something," Thomas said. "Mrs. Williams said that there are only four letters. So how can we have so many different proteins?"

"Well, let's play a game," Mrs. Love replied. "I will give you four letters. Make as many words from them as you can. The one who makes the most words wins. Your letters are T–E–A–M!"

"The students scrambled for pencil and paper and furiously started scribbling in their notebooks. When the time was up, Gabriella had the most words—6.

Mrs. Love praised the class' efforts. Most students had at least two words, and many had four or five. Tea—met—team—mat were the most common.

By having the students do the word exercise, Mrs. Love explained that they could come up with so many words using just four letters. She also asked the class to imagine how many more words they could make if they used some letters more than once! They might make T-E-A-M-M-A-T-E! That's what the genes do. They use the same four letters— A, C, G, and T- over and over again - to make so many wonderful protein codes. Mrs. Love promised to tell them more about protein codes in her next class.

"Wow! Genes are so important, and we did not know anything about them before. Not even their correct spelling. I'd better call Casey a cowinner of the spelling bee," said Gabriella.

Casey smiled and gave a thumbs-up!

FUN FACT

Remember, genes are just a part of DNA, although the most important part. The human **genome** consists of 3 billion letter pairs that make up our DNA. If you were to isolate the DNA from one human cell and stretch that open, it will stand six feet tall. And by some estimates, if you lined up all the DNA in our bodies from end to end, it would be long enough to stretch to the sun and back over 300 times, and moon around 150,000 times. Imagine that!

"There are so many fascinating and fun facts about genes," Mrs. Love said. "I will share a few with you and we can talk about more in our next few classes. Thank you Casey for asking about genes. I'm glad you did so we could learn about what the most important aspect of any living form truly is," continued Mrs. Love.

"By the way, you may not know this, but there is actually a National DNA Day. It is celebrated on April 25 every year", Mrs. Love shared.

FUN FACT

April 25th is celebrated as National DNA day. It's because that is the day, in 1953, when scientists James Watson, Francis Crick, Maurice Wilson, and Rosalind Franklin, along with their colleagues, published papers on the structure of DNA. The journal they published in was called *Nature*. That was a milestone moment in science.

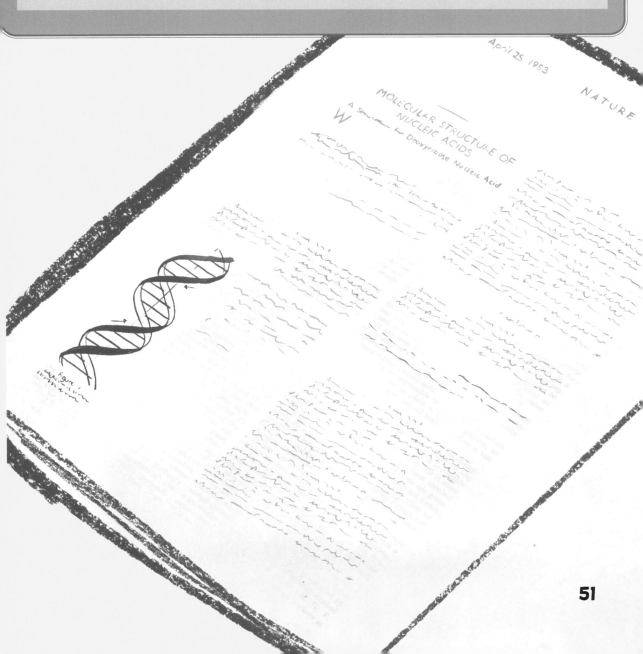

Anika, who was listening attentively, raised her hand and said, "Thank you, Mrs. Love, for telling us about the special day. I love special days. Just so that we are all clear, these scientists did what we did in Mrs. Williams's class. They drew the painting of DNA. Since we did the same thing, can we have our own School DNA Day?"

The entire class giggled.

Mrs. Love smiled. "I love the energy and enthusiasm in this class. It's awesome. Maybe we should have our School DNA Day.

"Boy, I am so happy that I did not spell 'genes' correctly. We learned so much about them," said Casey.

"Roger that!" chimed in Gabriella. "I never realized that such a small word could be so powerful," she continued.

"I already feel like a G–E–N–E–ius after learning so much from you and Mrs. Williams," said Thomas, smirking. The class cherished his clever pun.

Anika raised her hand and said, with her usual enthusiasm, "Thank you, thank you, thank you, Mrs. Love. Just so that we are all clear remember, I took notes in class that I will share with you all. Think of my notes as the building blocks of science class. I will call my journal *'Jackets and Genes'*. Jackets suggest phenotype and all the genes genotype. If anyone forgets what Mrs. Love and Mrs. Williams taught us, you can always read this journal. It is like an instruction book to understand genes."

"Thank YOU for being such a terrific and curious class!" Mrs. Love said. "The next time we get together, let's talk about gnomes . . . er, I mean genomes. Maybe even 'Gnomes and Genomes.' I can't wait to teach you more about this next time!"

GLOSSARY

(Glossary source: Courtesy: National Human Genome Research Institute. Additional resources can be found at https://www.genome.gov)
Terms:
ACGT/ Base pair/ Cell/ Chromosome/ DNA/ Double Helix/ Gene/ Genetic Code/ /Genome/Genotype/ Human Genome Project/ Nucleotide/ Nucleus/ Phenotype/ Protein

ACGT:

ACGT is an acronym for the four types of bases found in a DNA molecule: adenine (A), cytosine (C), guanine (G), and thymine (T). A DNA molecule consists of two strands wound around each other, with each strand held together by bonds between the bases. Adenine pairs with thymine, and cytosine pairs with guanine.

BASE PAIR:

A base pair is two chemical bases bonded to one another forming a "rung of the DNA ladder." The DNA molecule consists of two strands that wind around each other like a twisted ladder. Each strand has a backbone made of alternating sugar (deoxyribose) and phosphate groups. Attached to each sugar is one of four bases--adenine (A), cytosine (C), guanine (G), or thymine (T).

CELL:

A cell is the basic building block of living things. An adult human body is estimated to contain between 10 and 100 trillion cells.

CHROMOSOME:

A chromosome is an organized package of DNA found in the nucleus of the cell. Different organisms have different numbers of chromosomes. Humans have 23 pairs of chromosomes. Each parent contributes one chromosome to each pair so that children get half of their chromosomes from their mother and half from their father.

DNA (deoxyribo nucleic acid):

DNA is the chemical name for the molecule that carries genetic instructions in all living things. The DNA molecule consists of two strands that wind around one another to form a shape known as a double helix. Each strand has a backbone made of alternating sugar (deoxyribose) and phosphate groups. Attached to each sugar is one of four bases--adenine (A), cytosine (C), guanine (G), and thymine (T).

DOUBLE HELIX:

Double helix is the description of the structure of a DNA molecule. A DNA molecule consists of two strands that wind around each other like a twisted ladder. Each strand has a backbone made of alternating groups of sugar (deoxyribose) and phosphate groups. Attached to each sugar is one of four bases: adenine (A), cytosine (C), guanine (G), or thymine (T).

GENE:

The gene is the basic physical unit of inheritance. Genes are passed from parents to offspring and contain the information needed to specify traits (or properties). Genes are arranged, one after another, on structures called chromosomes. A chromosome contains a single, long DNA molecule, only a portion of which corresponds to a single gene. Humans have approximately 20,000 genes arranged on their chromosomes. The sequence of bases in a portion of a DNA molecule, called a gene, carries the instructions needed to assemble a protein.

GENETIC CODE:

The instructions in a gene that tell the cell how to make a specific protein. A, C, G, and T are the "letters" of the DNA code; they stand for the chemicals adenine (A), cytosine (C), guanine (G), and thymine (T), respectively, that make up the nucleotide bases of DNA. Each gene's code combines the four chemicals in various ways to spell out three-letter "words" that specify which amino acid is needed at every step in making a protein.

GENOME:

The genome is the entire set of genetic instructions found in a cell. In humans, the genome consists of 23 pairs of chromosomes, found in the nucleus, as well as a small chromosome found in the cells' mitochondria. Each set of 23 chromosomes contains approximately 3.1 billion bases of DNA sequence.

GENOTYPE:

A genotype is an individual's collection of genes. The term also can refer to the two alleles inherited for a particular gene. The genotype is expressed when the information encoded in the genes' DNA is used to make protein and RNA molecules. The expression of the genotype contributes to the individual's observable traits, called the phenotype.

HUMAN GENOME PROJECT:

The Human Genome Project was an international project that mapped and sequenced the entire human genome. Completed in April 2003, data from the project are freely available to researchers and others interested in genetics and human health.

NUCLEOTIDE:

A nucleotide is the basic building block of nucleic acids. A nucleotide consists of a sugar molecule (either ribose in RNA or deoxyribose in DNA) attached to a phosphate group and a nitrogen-containing base. The bases used in DNA are adenine (A), cytosine (C), guanine (G), and thymine (T). In RNA, the base uracil (U) takes the place of thymine.

NUCLEUS:

A nucleus is a membrane-bound organelle that contains the cell's chromosomes. Pores in the nuclear membrane allow for the passage of molecules in and out of the nucleus.

PHENOTYPE:

A phenotype is an individual's observable traits, such as height, eye color, and blood type. The genetic contribution to the phenotype is called the genotype. Some traits are largely determined by the genotype, while other traits are largely determined by environmental factors.

PROTEIN:

Proteins are an important class of molecules found in all living cells. A protein is composed of one or more long chains of amino acids, the sequence of which corresponds to the DNA sequence of the gene that encodes it. Proteins play a variety of roles in the cell, including structural (cytoskeleton), mechanical (muscle), biochemical (enzymes), and cell signaling (hormones). Proteins are also an essential part of diet.

And, finally, we have the most important glossary term for you:

"VERY SPECIAL YOU!"

This is what you are. A unique and amazing person. There is no one as distinct as you are, truly special!!

Deepak Asudani MD, MPH

Deepak is a Professor of Medicine at University of California, San Diego, CA, where he sees patients and teaches clinical medicine. He has a keen interest in applied genomics, and precision medicine. In his spare time, he likes being with his family and dogs and tending his garden. For more details, please visit https://www.linkedin.com/in/dgasudani/. Deepak's favorite part in the book is: "When Thomas paints his beautiful version of DNA".

Ananya Asudani

Ananya is an 8th grader at Oak Valley Middle School in San Diego, CA. She hopes to continue to blend her storytelling and creative writing skills with her fascination for science to write about STEM disciplines. A competitive soccer player, she aspires to be either an entrepreneur or a women's rights attorney. In her free time, she loves to play with her dogs – Griffin (featured in this book) and Teddy (you will meet him later). Ananya's favorite part of this book is: "When Anika, Casey, Gabriella, and Thomas along with Griffin are sitting on school steps to find out what genes are".

Aarnav Asudani

Aarnav is a 4th grader at Stone Ranch Elementary School in San Diego, CA. He has always been fascinated by science, geography and math. For no clear reasons, at the age of 8, he decided to understand the central dogma of genetic information - nucleotide base pairing, replication, transcription and translation. His career choices change by the week, if not daily. At this time, he aspires to be either an engineer, inventor, or a scientist – and ideally all of these. Aarnav's favorite part of this book is: "When Casey imagines sliding down the cool DNA helix in Mrs. Williams' class".

ABOUT THE ILLUSTRATOR

Katie Risor

Katie Risor is a children's author, illustrator and designer living and working in Texas. She's worked on books such as *Casey's Kite*, *There's an Alligator in the Elevator!* and more! Growing up on heartfelt fantasy like *The NeverEnding Story*, *Mary Poppins*; storybooks like *Winnie the Pooh*; and playing outside every day with her friends, led Katie to create art and stories inspired by nature, everyday experiences and a little bit of magic. Her favorite part of this book is the art class scene. You can find more of Katie's work at her website **www.katierisor.com** and on social media.

Lightning Source UK Ltd.
Milton Keynes UK
UKHW052146270223
417762UK00003B/114